2010 Joint United States-Canadian Program to Explore the Limits of the Extended Continental Shelf Aboard U.S. Coast Guard Cutter *Healy*—Cruise HLY1002

August 2–September 6, 2010

Dutch Harbor to Barrow, Alaska

By Brian D. Edwards, Jonathan R. Childs, Peter J. Triezenberg, William W. Danforth, and Helen Gibbons

Open-File Report 2013–1067

U.S. Department of the Interior
U.S. Geological Survey

U.S. Department of the Interior
SALLY JEWELL, Secretary

U.S. Geological Survey
Suzette M. Kimball, Acting Director

U.S. Geological Survey, Reston, Virginia: 2013

For more information on the USGS—the Federal source for science about the Earth,
its natural and living resources, natural hazards, and the environment—visit
http://www.usgs.gov or call 1–888–ASK–USGS

For an overview of USGS information products, including maps, imagery, and publications,
visit http://www.usgs.gov/pubprod.

To order this and other USGS information products, visit http://store.usgs.gov .

Contents

Figures

Tables

Conversion Factors

Inch/Pound to SI

Multiply	By	To obtain
Mass		
pound, avoirdupois (lb)	0.4536	kilogram (kg)
Length		
mile, nautical (nmi)	1.852	kilometer (km)

SI to Inch/Pound

Multiply	By	To obtain
Length		
meter (m)	3.281	foot (ft)
kilometer (km)	0.6214	mile (mi)
kilometer (km)	0.5400	mile, nautical (nmi)
meter (m)	1.094	yard (yd)
Area		
square kilometer (km^2)	247.1	acre
Flow rate		
meter per second (m/s)	3.281	foot per second (ft/s)
Acceleration		
milligal (mGal)	100	meter per second per second (m/s^2)

2010 Joint United States-Canadian Program to Explore the Limits of the Extended Continental Shelf Aboard U.S. Coast Guard Cutter *Healy*—Cruise HLY1002

August 2—September 6, 2010

Dutch Harbor to Barrow, Alaska

By Brian D. Edwards, Jonathan R. Childs, Peter J. Triezenberg, William W. Danforth, and Helen Gibbons

Abstract

In August and September 2010, the U.S. Geological Survey, in cooperation with Natural Resources Canada, Geological Survey of Canada, conducted bathymetric and geophysical surveys in the Beaufort Sea and eastern Arctic Ocean aboard the U.S. Coast Guard Cutter *Healy*. The principal objective of this mission to the high Arctic was to acquire data in support of a delineation of the outer limits of the U.S. and Canadian Extended Continental Shelf in the Arctic Ocean, in accordance with the provisions of Article 76 of the United Nations Convention on the Law of the Sea.

The *Healy* was accompanied by the Canadian Coast Guard icebreaker *Louis S. St-Laurent*. The scientific parties on board the two vessels consisted principally of staff from the U.S. Geological Survey (*Healy*), and the Geological Survey of Canada and the Canadian Hydrographic Service (*Louis*). The crew also included marine-mammal observers, Native-community observers, ice observers, and biologists conducting research of opportunity in the Arctic Ocean.

Despite interruptions necessitated by three medical emergencies, the joint survey proved largely successful. The *Healy* collected 7,201 trackline-kilometers of swath (multibeam) bathymetry (47,663 square kilometers) and CHIRP subbottom data, with accompanying marine gravity measurements, and expendable bathythermograph data. The *Louis* acquired 3,673 trackline-kilometers of multichannel seismic (airgun) deep-penetration reflection data along 25 continuous profiles, as well as 34 sonobuoy refraction stations and 9,500 trackline-kilometers of single-beam bathymetry. The coordinated efforts of the two vessels resulted in seismic-reflection-profile data that were of much higher quality and continuity than if the data had been acquired with a single vessel alone. The equipment-failure rate of the seismic equipment aboard the *Louis* was greatly reduced when the *Healy* led as the ice breaker. When ice conditions proved too severe to deploy the seismic system, the *Louis* led the *Healy*, resulting in much improved quality of the swath bathymetric and CHIRP subbottom data in comparison with data collected either by the *Healy* in the lead or the *Healy* working alone.

During periods when the *Healy* was operating alone (principally when the *Louis* was diverted for emergency medical evacuations or ship repairs), the *Healy* was able to deploy a piston-core-sampler (10 meters maximum potential recovery depending on configuration). The coring operations resulted in recovery of cores at five locations ranging from 2.4 to 5.7 meters in length from water depths ranging from 1,157 to 3,700 meters. One of these cores sited on the Alaskan margin recovered the first reported occurrence of methane hydrate from the Arctic Ocean.

Ancillary science objectives, including ice observations and deployment of ice-monitoring buoys and water-column sampling to measure acidification of Arctic waters were successfully conducted. The water-column sampling included using 10 full-ocean-depth, water-sampling casts with accompanying conductivity-temperature-depth measurements.

Except for the data deemed proprietary, data from the cruise have been archived and are available for download at the National Geophysical Data Center and at cooperating organizations.

Outreach staff and guest teachers aboard the two vessels provided near-real-time connection between the research activities and the public through online blogs, web pages, and other media.

Introduction

In August and September 2010, the U.S. Geological Survey (USGS), in cooperation with Natural Resources Canada, Geological Survey of Canada (GSC), conducted bathymetric and geophysical surveys in the Arctic Beaufort Sea and Canada Basin aboard the U.S. Coast Guard (USCG) Cutter *Healy* under the command of Capt. William (Bill) J. Rall. The principal objective of this mission (USCG identifier HLY1002; USGS Field Activity ID: H-3-10-AR) to the high Arctic was to acquire data in support of a delineation of the outer limits of the Extended Continental Shelf (ECS) beyond the 200-nmi-wide Exclusive Economic Zone (EEZ) in the Arctic Ocean in accordance with the provisions of Article 76 of the United Nations Convention on the Law of the Sea (see *http://www.un.org/Depts/los/index.htm*).

The *Healy* was accompanied by the Canadian Coast Guard icebreaker *Louis S. St-Laurent* (survey identifier LSSL2012; fig. 1). The scientific parties on board the two vessels consisted principally of staff from the USGS (*Healy*), and the GSC and the Canadian Hydrographic Service (*Louis*). The crew included marine-mammal observers, Native-community observers, ice observers, and oceanographers conducting research of opportunity in the Arctic Ocean.

Figure 1. Photo showing U.S. Coast Guard Cutter *Healy* and Canadian Coast Guard icebreaker *Louis S. St-Laurent* (*Louis*) breaking through ice in the Arctic Beaufort Sea.

The *Healy* departed Dutch Harbor, Alaska, on August 2, 2010; the *Louis* departed Kugluktuk, Nunavut, Canada, on August 6, 2010. Upon arrival in the operation area on August 8 (dates and times are in Coordinated Universal Time [UTC] "-7" unless noted otherwise), the *Healy* spent 2 days conducting a single-vessel multibeam bathymetric survey near longitude 141°W, a zone of mutual interest to the U.S. and Canada. During this time, the *Louis'* scientific party deployed and tested airgun seismic-reflection gear in open water. The two vessels rendezvoused on August 11, and proceeded west to commence the seismic survey in the U.S. Exclusive Economic Zone (EEZ). However, after only a few hours, a crewmember on board the *Louis* was injured. The *Louis* suspended the seismic survey and transited to Tuktoyuktuk, Canada, for the medical evacuation (medevac). During this 2-day medevac by the *Louis*, the *Healy* conducted coring operations along the Beaufort margin and recovered one gravity core and two piston cores (see section, "Geological Sampling" for details). The two vessels rejoined on August 13 and conducted seismic surveys in the U.S. EEZ. When clear of the ice pack on August 16, the *Healy* left the *Louis* and transited to Barrow, Alaska, to pick up a replacement engineer and engine room parts for the *Louis*; the *Healy* rejoined the *Louis* on August 17, and the vessels continued joint operations within the U.S. EEZ. Throughout the joint operations, the *Healy* typically led the *Louis* during seismic-reflection profiling, while the *Louis* led the *Healy* when heavy ice conditions precluded deployment of the seismic-reflection system, incidentally resulting in significant improvement of the multibeam data quality (fig. 2).

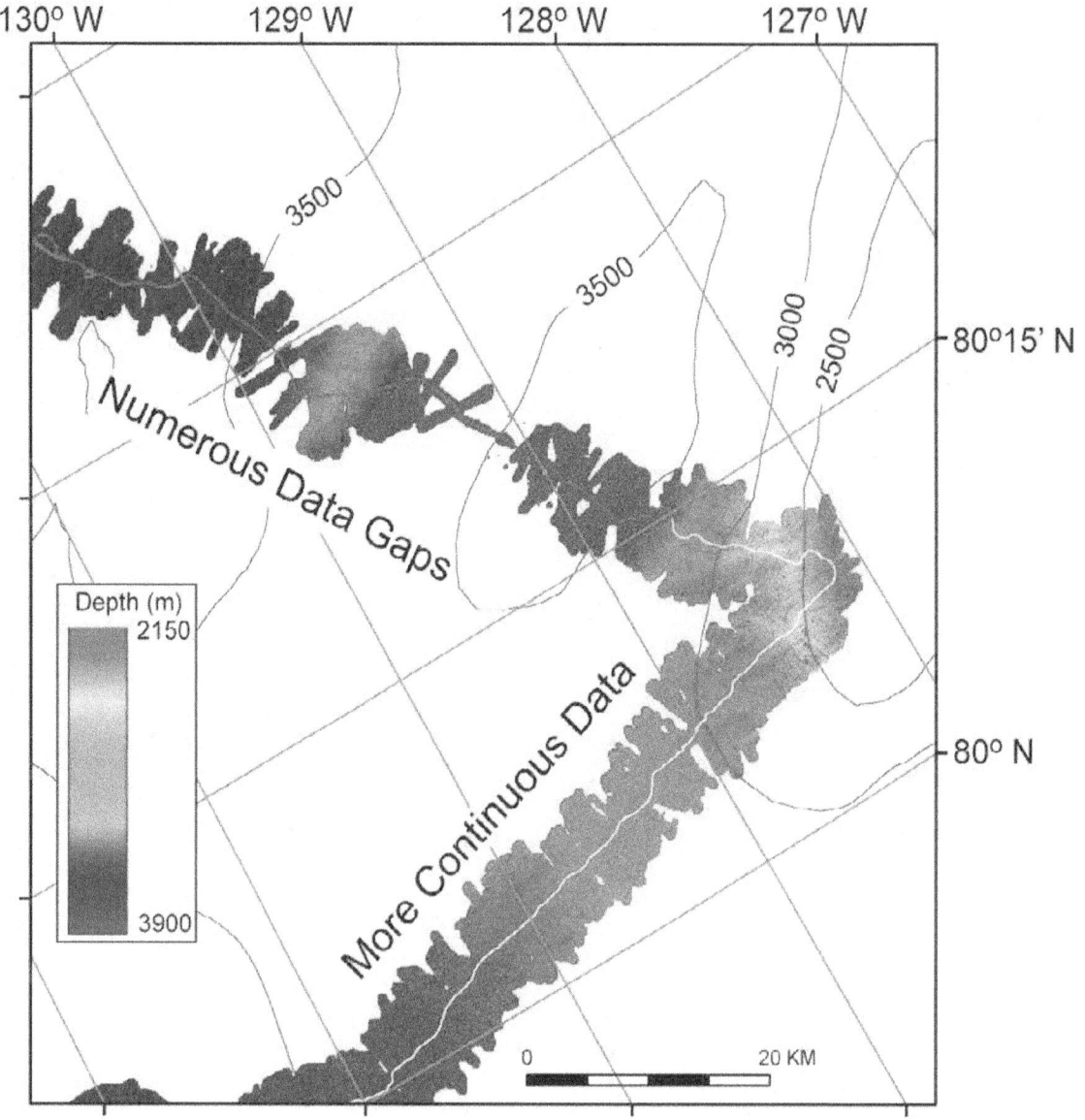

Figure 2. Figure illustrating the quality of *Healy* swath multibeam data coverage in 2008. Red trackline along the swath centerbeam identifies *Healy* breaking ice in front of *Louis*. White trackline along the centerbeam identifies *Louis* breaking ice in front of *Healy*. Note the marked improvement in swath continuity and width when *Healy* was the trailing vessel.

Early in the morning on August 24, the *Louis* was forced to stop data collection owing to a damaged bearing on her port drive shaft assembly. After determining the nature of the damage and the *Louis'* safety, the *Healy* steamed alone to the site of the 2009 seamount discovery (Mayer and Armstrong, 2009), conducted a survey, and, unable to dredge because of ice conditions, recovered a piston core from a sediment pond on the upper flank of the seamount. The vessels rejoined midday on August 26, and continued joint operations until a medical emergency aboard the *Louis* on August 29 necessitated a second medevac. For 2 days, the ships convoyed south through heavy ice with the *Healy* typically leading the way. On August 30, shortly after clearing the heavy ice, an injury to a *Healy* crew member required transport to the *Louis*. The *Louis* then proceeded alone to Tuktoyuktuk, Canada, with both injured personnel. Between August 30 and September 2, the *Healy* conducted coring operations off the Canadian continental margin. The ships met again on September 3 and conducted joint seismic survey operations until early evening on September 4 when the two ships parted. The *Healy* returned to Barrow, Alaska, on September 6, and the *Louis* returned to Kugluktuk, Canada, on September 15 (fig. 3). Detailed trackline navigation for the two ships is presented in figure 4. Mosher and others (2011) compiled a cruise report for the *Louis* leg of the mission.

USGS activities in mapping the ECS are coordinated through the U.S. Extended Continental Shelf Task Force, which is composed of representatives from the USGS, the U.S. Department of State, the National Oceanographic and Atmospheric Administration (NOAA), and several other governmental agencies. Further information on the task force and its activities is posted at *http://www.continentalshelf.gov/*.

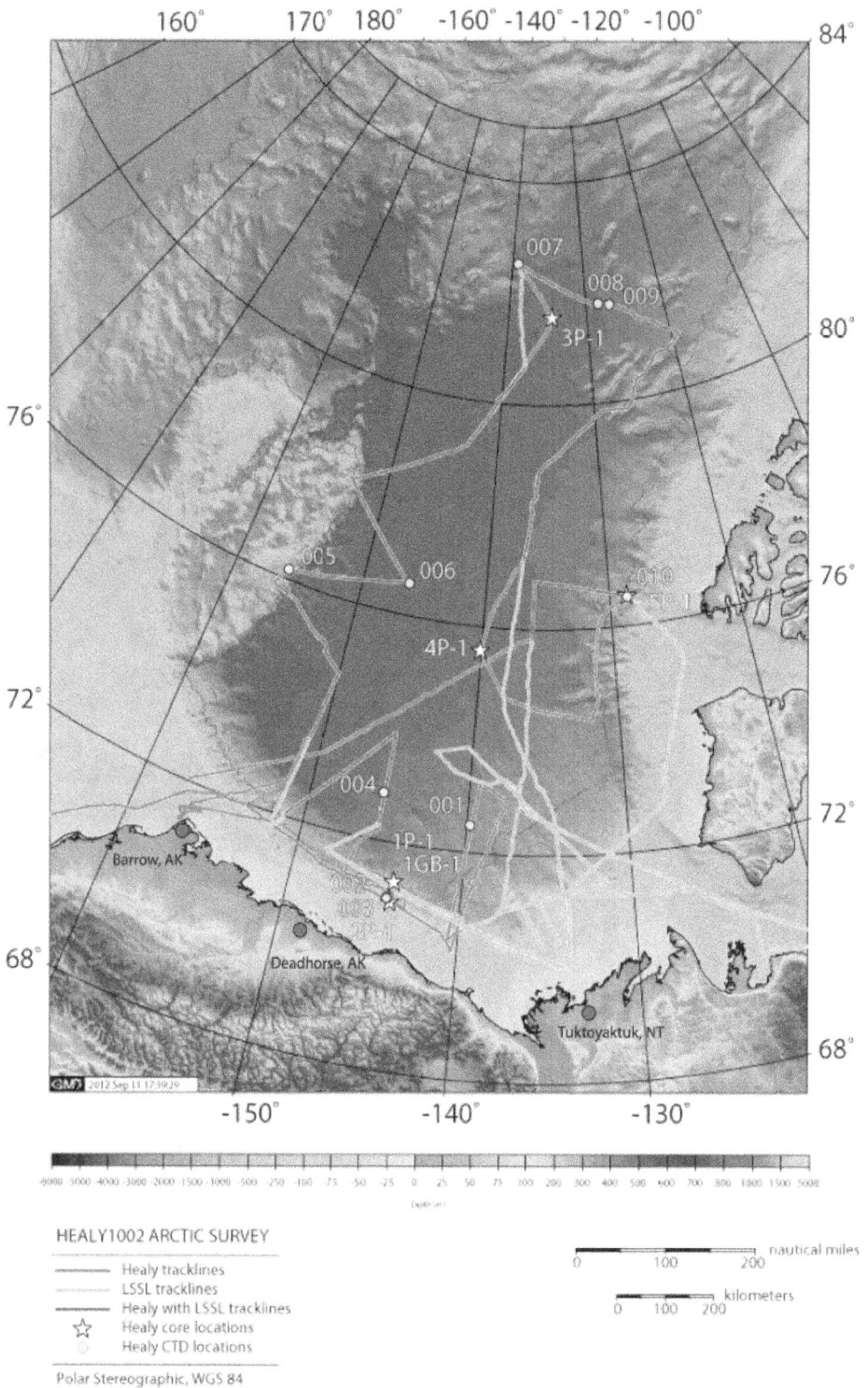

Figure 3. Map showing tracklines for *Healy* (red) and *Louis* (yellow), and when both vessels were in convoy (purple). Stars indicate the location of coring sites; circles indicate the location of conductivity-temperature-depth rosette casts (with station identification number) done from *Healy*.

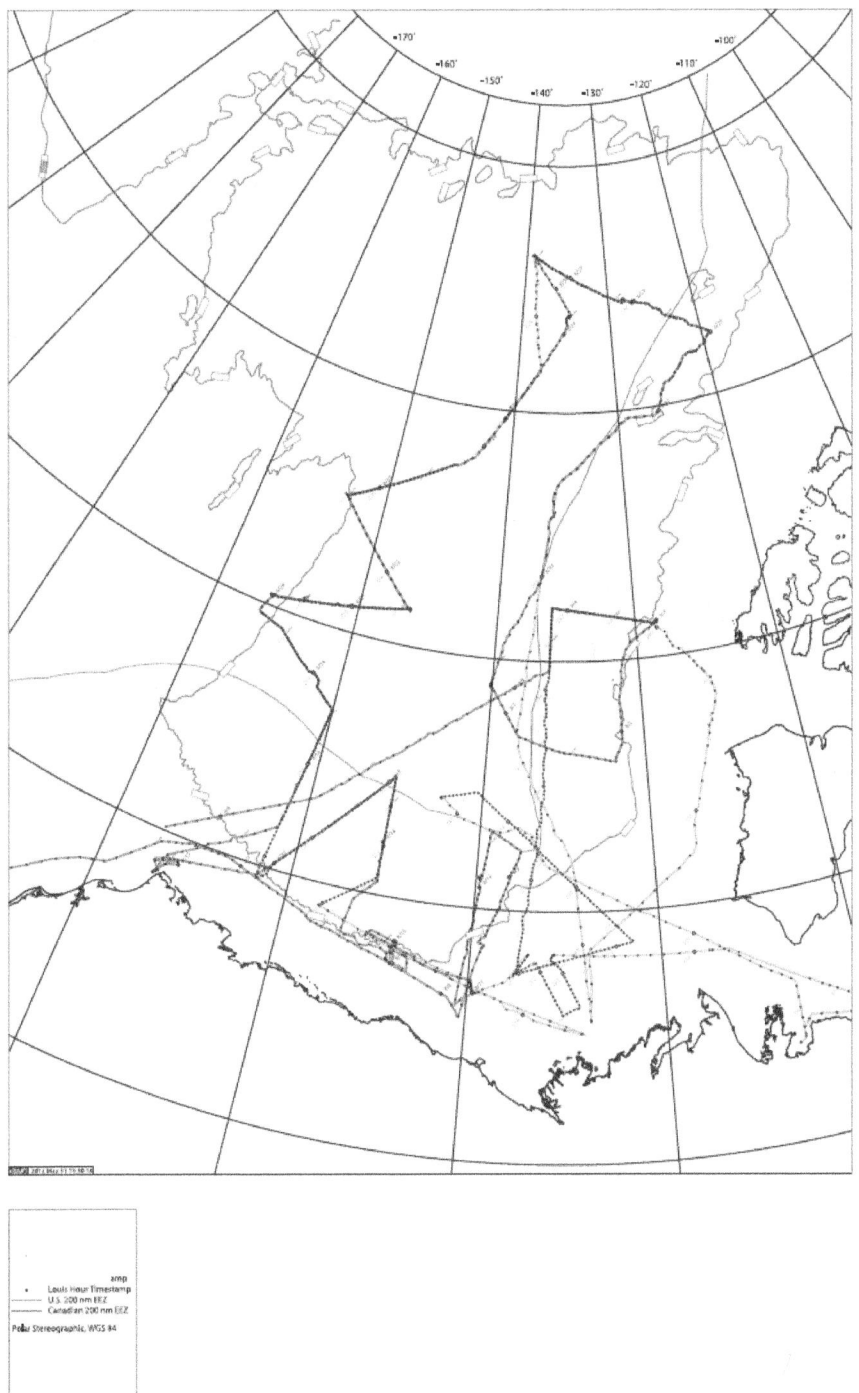

Figure 4. Map showing trackline locations for *Healy* (red) and *Louis* (yellow). Clicking on the figure will bring up a full resolution view of the tracklines revealing the relative position of each vessel. The tracks for both ships are annotated every hour - *Healy* tracks are annotated with month/day and *Louis* tracks are annotated with day-of-the-year (the conventions used to record dates on the respective vessels). U.S. and Canadian EEZ boundaries are shown for reference. NOTE: the swath bathymetry and subbottom profile data acquired during HLY1002 within the Canadian 200-nautical-mile-wide EEZ are proprietary and public release is not authorized at this time. See section, "Data and Metadata" for further details.

Previous Surveys

This joint U.S.-Canadian program, started in 2008, was built on earlier work by both countries. The USGS (with Canadian participation) conducted geophysical surveys in 1988, 1991, and 1992 in the Arctic aboard the USCG icebreaker *Polar Star* (Grantz and others, 2004).

Seismic reflection and refraction data were acquired in the Arctic from the *Healy* in 2005 (cruise HLY0503; Coakley and others, 2005) and 2006 (cruise HLY0602). These surveys were funded by the National Science Foundation, and were not associated with or funded through the U.S. Extended Continental Shelf Task Force. Further details are available at Coakley and others (2005) and posted at the following URLs:

http://icefloe.net/healy-2005-cruise-reports
http://icefloe.net/healy-2006-cruise-reports

In 2003, 2004, 2007, and 2008, the University of New Hampshire Center for Coastal and Ocean Mapping and the NOAA Joint Hydrographic Center conducted a series of bathymetric surveys with the *Healy* funded by the U.S. ECS program (Mayer, 2003, 2004; Mayer and Armstrong, 2007, 2008).

In 2007, the GSC and the Canadian Hydrographic Service conducted geophysical and bathymetric surveys aboard the *Louis* in the Arctic in single-vessel mode. As of March, 2013, the data from this survey are proprietary.

The joint U.S.-Canadian Arctic program was initiated in 2008 (Hutchinson and others, 2009; Jackson and DesRoches, 2010; Childs and others, 2012) and continued in 2009 (Mayer and Armstrong, 2009; Mosher and others, 2009). After the 2010 expedition reported here, a fourth and final joint survey was conducted in 2011 (Mayer and Armstrong, 2011; Mosher, 2012).

Scientific Party

Members of the 2010 HLY1002 scientific party are listed in table 1 with each individual's institutional association and position on the cruise.

Table 1. HLY1002 scientific party.

HLY1002 science party		
Name	**Institution**	**Position**
Brian D. Edwards	USGS	Chief Scientist
Kwasi Addae	MRAG	Protected Species Observer
Sarah Ashworth	MRAG	Protected Species Observer
Tom Bolmer	WHOI/LDEO/ NSF	Data Specialist
Michel Bourdeau	Captain, Canadian Coast Guard	Canadian command liaison
Dale Chayes	LDEO/NSF	Science Systems
Jonathan Childs	USGS	USGS liaison (aboard *Louis*)
Erin Clark	Canadian Ice Service - Environment Canada	Ice Services Specialist
Pablo Clemente-Colon	NIC/NOAA	Scientist
Pete dal Ferro	USGS	Engineering Technician
William Danforth	USGS	Scientist
Christopher Dufore	USGS	Scientist
Helen Gibbons	USGS	Scientist
Donny Graham	ESU	Internet Technician
Ralph Kaleak	BASC	Native Community Liaison
Sherwood Liu	USF	Scientist
Joshua Miller	NIC/USCG	Ice Analyst/Buoy Technician
Thomas O'Brien	USGS	Scientist
Caryn Panowicz	NIC	Ice analyst (aboard *Louis*)
Mark Patsavas	USF	Scientist
Justin Pudenz	MRAG	Protected Species Observer
Steve Roberts	NCAR/LDEO/ NSF	Computer engineer
William Schmoker	PolarTREC Arctic Research Consortium	Teacher outreach
Caroline Singler	NOAA/Teacher- at-Sea	Teacher outreach
Andrew Stevenson	USGS	Scientist
David Street	Canadian Hydrographic Service	Hydrogropher
Peter Triezenberg	USGS	Scientist
Jenny White	USGS	Engineering Technician

Acronym	Institution
BASC	Barrow Arctic Science Consortium
ESU	Electronic Systems Support Unit Seattle
LDEO	Lamont-Doherty Earth Observatory, Columbia University
MRAG	MRAG Americas
NCAR	NOAA National Center for Atmospheric Research
NIC	NOAA National Ice Center
NOAA	National Oceanic and Atmospheric Association
NSF	National Science Foundation
USCG	U.S. Coast Guard
USF	University of South Florida
USGS	U.S. Geological Survey
WHOI	Woods Hole Oceanographic Institution

Underway Geophysical Data Acquisition and Processing

Complete details of all geophysical, oceanographic, and meteorologic sensors aboard the *Healy* are presented in appendix C, the onboard data synopsis is by technical staff members Dale Chayes, Steve Roberts, and Tom Bolmer.

During the cruise, data acquisition was synchronized to Greenwich Mean Time (equivalent to Coordinated Universal Time [UTC]). During two-ship operations, both vessels synchronized their clocks to UTC minus 7 hours (Pacific Daylight Time). Prior to the rendezvous with the *Louis* and following the final separation from the *Louis*, the *Healy's* ship clocks were set to UTC minus 8 hours (Alaska Daylight Time).

The *Healy* is equipped with a Kongsberg EM122 echosounder and a Knudsen 320 B/R bottom sounder, both hull mounted. Two Bell BGM-3 gravimeters were installed for the cruise in the vessel's IC Gyro compartment. The quality of these datasets varied widely, depending on ice conditions and ship operations.

Data acquisition was monitored continuously throughout the cruise by scientific and technical watchstanders. The scientific watchstanders worked 8-hour watches (00:00–08:00, 08:00–16:00, and 16:00–24:00, local ship time) and were responsible for monitoring all underway equipment. During each watch, the watchstanders would adjust acquisition parameters for the Kongsberg and Knudsen systems, ensure that data files were being updated, note anomalies or changes in operations in the e-log, and inform the ship technical staff when an instrument malfunctioned.

Although minor malfunctions occasionally interrupted data acquisition, these data gaps typically occurred for no more than a few minutes. No major instrument failures of the multibeam or subbottom profilers occurred during the cruise.

Multibeam Swath Bathymetry

Acquisition

Multibeam echosounder data were collected onboard the *Healy* using a Kongsberg EM122 echosounder that is permanently installed on the hull. Data were acquired on a PC workstation running the SIS software acquisition package supplied by Kongsberg. Each sensor offset, such as the location of the navigation antennas and the actual location of the motion reference unit, were measured from a common reference point. These values were entered to the data acquisition system prior to survey operations, and ensured that the sensor data streams were properly applied to the multibeam data during acquisition. Raw data were saved to disk in Kongsberg's "raw.all" format (Kongsberg, 2010).

Primary navigation and motion data (heave, pitch, roll, heading) were measured with an Applanix POS/MV-320 system, and these data were integrated with the multibeam data acquisition, ensuring that the ship's motion was compensated for and applied to the data in real time. Navigational data from the POS/MV-320 were incorporated in the multibeam data acquisition as well, and stored in the raw data files. Sound velocity at the keel (for the beamformer) was calculated from seawater temperature and conductivity as measured by an installed SeaBird SBE-45 Thermosalinograph. To ensure proper beam ray tracing through the water column during data acquisition, sound-velocity profiles were constructed from two sources: (1) data acquired by profiling systems deployed during the cruise, and (2) historical data. The deployed systems included expendable bathythermograph (XBT), conductivity-temperature-depth (CTD), and expendable conductivity-temperature-depth (XCTD) profiling systems; historical data were obtained from the Levitus database (see *http://iridl.ldeo.columbia.edu/SOURCES/.LEVITUS94/.dataset_documentation.html/*). Data were corrected for variations of sound velocity in the water column and for the draft of the multibeam transmit-receive arrays in real time by the sonar data-acquisition program, and were then saved to the raw data files.

Processing

The raw data files were brought into the CARIS HIPS and SIPS 7.0 software (see *http://www.caris.com/products/hips-sips/*) using the CARIS conversion wizard, which converts all data packets in the raw Kongsberg multibeam files to the internal CARIS format. Before the conversion was run, a vessel file named Healy2010_EM122.hvf was created with roll, pitch, heave, gyro, navigation and swath 1 activated within the file. This file is necessary for two reasons: (1) all converted files are stored in a named hierarchy that includes the vessel file name, and (2) the file identifies to CARIS the sensors that are to be parsed from the raw input file for visual inspection after conversion. As mentioned in section, "Acquisition," the SIS data acquisition program applied the heave, pitch, and roll data during acquisition; therefore, during the data conversion, the values for heave, pitch, roll, heading, and navigation were carried over into the converted CARIS files but not applied by the conversion process.

The converted data were stored on disk in a project folder (HealyAugust2010) that contains a subfolder named after the vessel file (Healy2010_EM122). That subfolder was further subdivided into Julian days, with each Julian-day folder containing all the line files for that day. For example, the *Healy* 1002 CARIS database has this structure: HealyAugust2010/Healy2010_EM122/2010-219/line files.

The raw data were stored in filenames of the form LLLL_YYYYMMDD_HHMMSS_Healy.all, where LLLL is the line number, YYYYMMDD is the calendar date and HHMMSS is the time in UTC. The raw data were then transferred from the data server and converted to CARIS-readable format. Each 30-minute interval of the Julian day was saved with a unique file_id in the corresponding project and vessel folders.

The Universal North Polar Stereographic Projection system was used for the project map projection. A central meridian of -160°, latitude of true-scale 75°N., and the WGS84 ellipsoid were selected for the projection parameters to correspond with parameters used by other projects in the Arctic Law of the Sea program. The file mapdef.dat, was replaced with a file that resides in a HIPS/System directory to ensure that the Universal North Polar Stereographic Projection would plot correctly.

Swath editing first was performed manually to each line, and obviously erroneous soundings were removed from the data files. Auxiliary-sensor-data were not cleaned during processing because those corrections were applied during acquisition. Sound-velocity corrections were not applied during processing because these corrections were applied during the data-acquisition stage as well. Because tide loading is a mandatory step in the CARIS processing workflow, a file zerotide.tid was created for this survey with a zero tide value for the entire cruise, as no tidal data were available for the Arctic. Navigation and tide corrections were applied to each observed and edited sounding as the last step in the processing workflow.

A CARIS BASE surface (grid) then was generated as a first view to visually inspect the data quality and to further remove bad soundings if needed. A horizontal resolution of 100 m per grid node was used when creating the grid.

Each grid was examined (using the swath editor, if necessary) to identify and remove erroneous soundings that may have been missed on the first editing pass. Once these soundings were removed from the data files, the grid was recomputed to reflect the editing. Data gaps ("holes") in the grid were then filled by a mean-value interpolation using the average of neighboring pixels.

The final step in the processing work flow was to convert the grid into Fledermaus dtm/geo files for three-dimensional presentation of the collected data.

CTD/XBT

XBT casts were conducted at regular intervals throughout the cruise to establish sound-velocity profiles required to correct the multibeam bathymetry. Additionally, CTD casts, during which water samples also were collected, were made as time and operational schedules permitted. The CTD and XBT data acquisition is detailed in tables A.2 and A.3 of appendix B.

CHIRP Subbottom Profiler

Acquisition

The Knudsen BR-320 bottom sounder and subbottom profiler functioned well in the ice, maintaining a lock on the bottom even under heavy ice conditions. The primary effect of heavy ice was to introduce gaps in the profile data.

In addition to creating high-resolution subbottom reflection profiles using a frequency-modulated ("chirp") source signal, the Knudsen system tracks the bottom return, and generates a digital single-beam depth record. Unlike the Kongsberg system, however, which uses a dynamic sound-velocity-profile model to transform travel time to true depth, the Knudsen system uses a constant-velocity factor of 1,500 m/s. Therefore, digital depths from the Knudsen differ from and are less accurate than the Kongsberg centerbeam depths. The *Healy* also was equipped with an ODEC Bathy-2000 fathometer, which was not used during HLY1002.

Processing

See *http://sioseis.ucsd.edu/notes.html* for a discussion of Knudsen CHIRP systems and signal processing implemented on the *Healy*.

Sea Gravimeter Data

Two Bell BGR-3 gravimeters (BGM-221 and BGM-222) were installed on the *Healy* for the entire 2010 survey. Details of the installation and operation of these instruments are presented in appendix D of Mayer and Armstrong (2008).

The two gravimeters operated continuously during the period from the *Healy's* initial departure from Seattle, Washington, on May 16, 2010, until her return on October 12, 2010. Drift measurements for the two instruments were estimated over approximately 280 days, during which time the BGM-221 drifted imperceptibly (0.12 milligal) and the BGM-222 drifted slightly more (12.3 milligal).

The gravity field crossing errors in milligals, compared with those on other *Healy* cruises for the two gravimeters, are listed in table 2.

Table 2. Mis-ties (in milligals) at line crossings for two gravity meters (BGM-221, BGM-222) during four *Healy* Arctic cruises, 2008 to 2011.

	HLY-08-221	HLY-09-221	HLY-10-221	HLY-11-221	HLY-08-222	HLY-09-222	HLY-10-222	HLY-11-222
HLY-08-221	0.07	0.07	0.12	0.16	0.19	-0.03	0.34	0.17
HLY-09-221	0.08	0.08	-0.08	-0.04	0.05	-0.17	0.18	0.02
HLY-10-221	-0.12	0.08	0.01	0.01	-0.03	-0.21	0.13	-0.02
HLY-11-221	-0.16	0.04	0.02	0.02	0.12	-0.06	0.28	0.11
HLY-08-222	-0.19	-0.05	0.03	-0.12	0.05	0.05	0.29	0.07
HLY-09-222	0.03	0.17	0.21	0.06	0.03	0.03	0.46	0.25
HLY-10-222	-0.34	-0.18	-0.13	-0.28	-0.29	-0.46	0.11	0.11
HLY-11-222	-0.17	-0.02	0.02	-0.11	-0.07	-0.25	0.04	0.04

Acoustic Doppler Current Profilers (ADCP)

Both of the hull-mounted ADCPs (75 kilohertz and 150 kilohertz) operated continuously throughout the cruise. No interests in the ADCP measurements have been identified, on or off the ship, and, accordingly, these data were subjected to no further examination, processing, or quality control. The data are freely available for download and analysis by contacting the authors.

Geological Sampling

Throughout the 2010 cruise, the *Healy* occasionally operated alone— principally when the *Louis* was otherwise engaged in medevac transits or repairs. At these times, gravity and piston coring operations were conducted. As shown in figure 3 and detailed in table 3, coring occurred at five locations; the piston core system is shown in figure 5. One significant finding from these cores occurred at site 1P-1, where gas hydrate was recovered at a subbottom depth of 5.7 m. This is the first report of a methane hydrate sample recovered from the Arctic Basin-Ocean (Edwards and others, 2011).

USGS Piston Coring System on USCGC *Healy's* Fantail

Figure 5. Photograph showing piston coring system on aft deck of *Healy*.

The original coring target for site 1P-1 was a seafloor high on the continental slope northeast of Prudhoe Bay, Alaska, that had been identified from USGS multichannel seismic-reflection data acquired in 1977 (Grantz and others, 1982). Multibeam data collected during HLY1002, however, revealed a conical mound in the area of the original target (fig. 6), and the final coring site was shifted to the flank of that mound (water depth 2,538 m). The gas hydrate had a nodular and vein-filling morphology (fig. 7). Although the hydrate was not preserved, residual gas recovered from the core liner contained more than 95 percent methane by volume when corrected for atmospheric contamination (Hart and others, 2011). Other analyses and descriptions of these cores were presented by Edwards and others (2011) and Wan and others (2011).

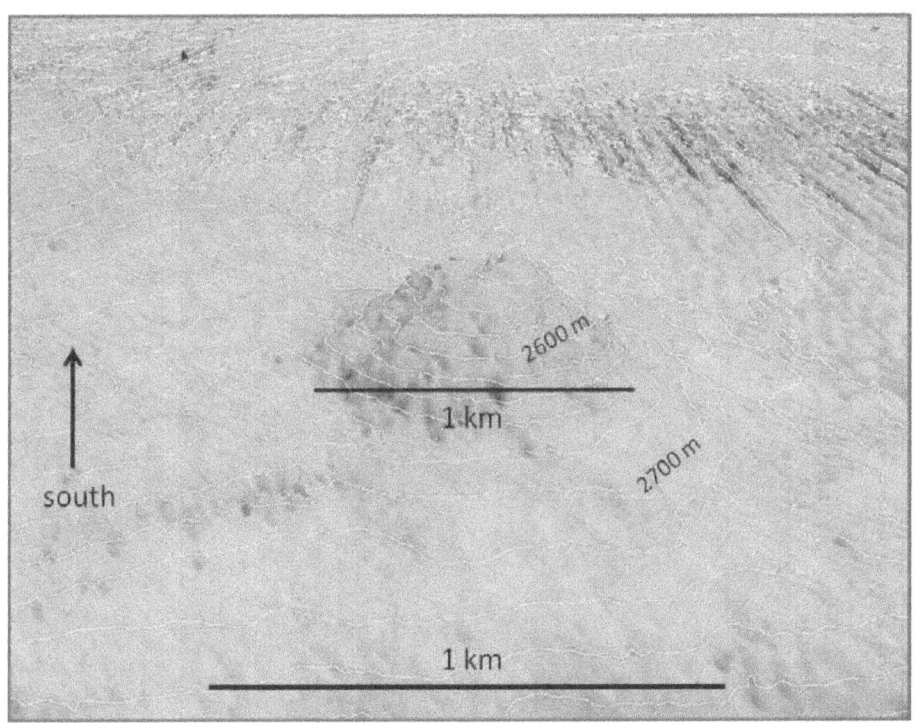

Figure 6. Multibeam bathymetric model showing hydrate mound with core sites indicated by red dots.

Figure 7. Photograph showing gas hydrate recovery in core catcher of piston core 1P-1.

Table 3. Details of coring locations, recovery, and subsamples taken.

SESAR_ISGN	Sample ID	Latitude N.	Longitude W.	Water Depth (m)	Equipment	Day	Time (UTC)	Recovery (cm)	Subsamples
ECS003000	1GB-1	71.31767°	143.99828°	2530	GB	8/11/2010	21:30	240	CC, MFx
ECS003001	1P-1	71.31747°	143.99970°	2538	P	8/12/2010	3:15	571	CA,CC,MFx, MFs
ECS003002	1TC-1	71.31747°	143.99970°	2538	TC	8/12/2010	3:15	83	CC,CA,MFx
ECS003003	2P-1	70.95910°	144.05238°	1157	P	8/12/2010	11:19	302	CC,CA,MFx
ECS003004	2TC-1	70.95910°	144.05238°	1157	TC	8/12/2010	11:19	79	CC,CA,MFx
ECS003005	3P-1	81.57966°	134.47790°	3070	P	8/25/2010	10:46	546	CC,CA(2),MFx, Tx
ECS003006	3TC-1	81.57966°	134.47790°	3070	TC	8/25/2010	10:46	NR	CA(2)
ECS003007	4P-1	75.58413°	140.09293°	3700	P	8/31/2010	12:54	337	CA,MFx
ECS003008	4TC-1	75.58413°	140.09293°	3700	TC	8/31/2010	12:54	NR	CA
ECS003009	5P-1	76.54377°	128.62745°	2081	P	9/2/2010	18:36	496	WSs,MFx,CA
ECS003010	5TC-1	76.54377°	128.62745°	2081	TC	9/2/2010	18:36	106	MFx,CA

Equipment

GB	Gravity Core (Big) 2,400 lb weightstand
P	Piston core (2,400 lb weightstand)
TC	Trigger core (part of piston core system)

Subsamples

CA	Core Catcher
CC	Core Cutter
MFs	microfauna surface sample
MFx	scrape of external pipe for microfauna
Tx	Texture sample
WSs	scrapings from weightstand head
NR	No recovery in main liner

SESAR_ISGN identifiers are assigned through the System for Earth SAmple Registration (SESAR): *http://www.geosamples.org/*

16

Ship Operations

A summary chronology of joint mission activities is presented in table 4.

Table 4. Chronology of ship operations during conduct of HLY1002 and LSSL2012.

[In column 1: 1, *Healy* was operating as a single vessel; 2, joint operations with *Healy* leading; 3, joint operations with *Louis* leading. DOY, Day of Year; EEZ, Exclusive Economic Zone; SOL, start of line; EOL, end of line; WP, way point; CTD, conductivity-temperature-depth; SVP, sound-velocity profile.]

Joint U.S.-Canada 2010 Arctic UNCLOS Program

Rev 11/7/2011

	Day of Week	Local Day	Local DOY	Local Time	UTC DOY	UTC (z)	UTC Delta	Vessel	Mission Chronology	Latitude N.	Longitude W.
1	M	2-Aug	214	15:00	214	23:00	-8	*Healy*	*Healy* departs Dutch Harbor		
1	W	4-Aug	216	16:00	216	21:00	-5	*Louis*	*Louis* crew exchange complete, Kugluktuk		
1	Tu	5-Aug	217		217		-5	*Louis*	*Louis* at anchor, Kugluktuk		
1	F	6-Aug	218	12:00	218	17:00	-5	*Louis*	*Louis* underway		
1	F	6-Aug	218	23:00	219	5:00	-6	*Louis*	Retard clocks one hour		
1	Sa	7-Aug	219	16:23	220	0:23	-8	*Healy*	Cross -141W; commence hydrographic survey of U.S.-Canada zone of mutual interest	70.55317°	141.00000°
1	Su	8-Aug	220	13:13	220	20:13	-7	*Louis*	SOL 1 deploy seismic gear open-water survey Canadian EEZ	71.18500°	135.71333°
1	Su	8-Aug	220	18:00	221	1:00	-7	*Healy*	Advance clocks one hour		
1	Su	8-Aug	220	23:00	221	6:00	-7	*Louis*	Retard clocks one hour		
1	Tu	10-Aug	222	8:35	222	15:35	-7	*Louis*	EOL 5 recover seismic gear open-water survey Canadian EEZ	71.31417°	136.99250°
1	Tu	10-Aug	222	17:30	223	0:30	-7	both	Rendezvous; Capt. Meeting (2 hours); transfer personnel; proceed in convoy toward U.S. EEZ		
1	W	10-Aug	222	22:54	223	5:54	-7	*Healy*	Cross -141W; finish hydrographic survey of U.S.-Canada zone of mutual interest; continue convoy	70.89583°	141.00000°

Joint U.S.-Canada 2010 Arctic UNCLOS Program

Rev 11/7/2011

	Day of Week	Local Day	Local DOY	Local Time	UTC DOY	UTC (z)	UTC Delta	Vessel	Mission Chronology	Latitude N.	Longitude W.
1	W	11-Aug	223	6:15	223	13:15	-7	Louis	Accident in Louis engine room necessitates transit to Tuktoyuktuk and medevac by helicopter		
1	W	11-Aug	223	6:30	223	13:30	-7	Healy	Proceeds alone within U.S. EEZ for sampling program		
1	W	11-Aug	223	13:30	223	20:30	-7	Healy	U.S. Incidental Harassment Authorization received by email		
1	W	11-Aug	223	14:30	223	21:30	-7	Healy	1GB-1 gravity core on bottom (depth =2,530 m)	71.31750°	143.99833°
1	W	11-Aug	223	15:00	223	22:00	-7	Louis	Marine Scientific Research Authorization received from U.S. Dept. of State for Louis to conduct science operations in U.S. EEZ		
1	W	11-Aug	223	19:18	224	2:18	-7	Healy	1P-1 piston core and 1TC-1 trigger core on bottom (depth = 2,538 m)	71.31750°	143.99967°
1	Th	12-Aug	224	4:20	224	11:20	-7	Healy	2P-1 piston core and 2TC-1 trigger core on bottom (depth = 1,157 m)	70.95917°	144.05233°
1	Th	12-Aug	224	16:07	224	23:07	-7	Louis	SOL 6 seismic in U.S. EEZ	71.65667°	148.18650°
2	F	13-Aug	225	7:20	225	14:20	-7	Healy	Healy joins Louis for SOL 7	72.26483°	145.40767°
1	Su	15-Aug	227	10:30	227	17:30	-7	Healy	Healy departs Louis in light ice to run to Barrow for crew and parts; continuing along Line 7 for multibeam and CHIRP		
1	M	16-Aug	228	14:20	228	21:20	-7	Healy	Supplies arrive Healy from Barrow; Dean Kavanaugh aboard Healy; Healy departs Barrow to resume escort	72.95650°	148.41383°
2	Tu	17-Aug	229	11:30	229	18:30	-7	Healy	Healy joins Louis at ice edge along Line 11	73.40883°	150.87883°

Joint U.S.–Canada 2010 Arctic UNCLOS Program

Rev 11/7/2011

	Day of Week	Local Day	Local DOY	Local Time	UTC DOY	UTC (z)	UTC Delta	Vessel	Mission Chronology	Latitude N.	Longitude W.
2	Tu	17-Aug	229	13:45	229	20:45	-7	Healy	Dean Kavanaugh and fuel filters depart *Healy* via helicopter en route to *Louis*		
2	Tu	17-Aug	229	22:50	230	5:50	-7	Louis	*Louis* exits U.S. EEZ	74.18333°	150.39333°
2	F	20-Aug	232	8:00	232	15:00	-7	Louis	EOL 14, seismic gear recovered for transit	76.58917°	146.41700°
1	F	20-Aug	232	9:00	232	16:00	-7	both	Both ships all stop for CTD/SVP (3 hrs)		
3	F	20-Aug	232	11:45	232	18:45	-7	Louis	Commence transit; *Louis* in lead		
2	Sa	21-Aug	233	4:42	233	11:42	-7	Louis	SOL 15, seismic gear deployed	78.11383°	153.27267°
2	Su	22-Aug	234	11:00	234	18:00	-7	Louis	EOL 16, seismic gear recovered for transit	78.97467°	145.28783°
3	M	23-Aug	235	15:00	235	22:00	-7	Louis	Commence transit; *Louis* in lead		
1	M	23-Aug	235	21:30	236	4:30	-7	Louis	*Louis* all stop to replace port shaft bearing		
1	M	23-Aug	235	22:50	236	5:50	-7	Healy	*Healy* departs escort with *Louis* and continues alone for seamount survey		
1	W	25-Aug	237	0:40	237	7:40	-7	Louis	*Louis* underway to rendezvous Healy (down 27 hours)		
1	W	25-Aug	237	10:46	237	17:46	-7	Healy	3P-1 piston core and 3TC-1 trigger core on bottom (depth = 3,070 m)	81.57133°	134.47783°
1	Th	26-Aug	238	3:00	238	10:00	-7	both	Rendezvous WP28 for W-E line	82.53000°	139.17833°
2	Th	26-Aug	238	4:30	238	11:40	-7	Louis	SOL 17, *Healy* in lead	82.54450°	138.93050°
1	F	27-Aug	239	8:00	239	15:30	-7	both	*Louis* retrieve seismic gear; all stop for CTD/SVP (5 hours)	81.78500°	128.30667°
1	F	27-Aug	239	15:00	239	22:00	-7	Louis	*Louis* retrieve seismic gear and repair; all stop (5 hours)		
3	F	27-	239	20:00	240	3:30	-7	both	Underway for bathymetric program, *Louis* in lead		

Joint U.S.-Canada 2010 Arctic UNCLOS Program

Rev 11/7/2011

	Day of Week	Local Day	Local DOY	Local Time	UTC DOY	UTC (z)	UTC Delta	Vessel	Mission Chronology	Latitude N.	Longitude W.
		Aug									
3	Sa	28-Aug	240	6:11	240	13:11	-7	Healy	Healy enters Canadian EEZ for MB bathymetry	81.38517°	122.99250°
3	Sa	28-Aug	240	18:00	241	1:00	-7	both	WP 29 in Canadian EEZ; health issue reported for steward aboard Louis - diverting S for medevac; Louis in lead with Healy following	80.98167°	119.07333°
1	Su	29-Aug	241		241		-7	both	Continue transit, vessels trade lead		
1	M	30-Aug	242	0:47	242	7:47	-7	Healy	Healy departs Canadian EEZ	79.51883°	131.64900°
1	M	30-Aug	242		242		-7	both	Continue transit, vessels trade lead		
1	M	30-Aug	242	9:45	242	16:45	-7	both	Vessels prepare to separate		
1	M	30-Aug	242	9:45	242	16:45	-7	Healy	Injury reported on Healy - crew member will require medical evacuation; vessels continue to convoy for U.S./Canada mainland		
1	M	30-Aug	242	11:15	242	18:15	-7	Healy	Injured Healy crew member transferred by launch to Louis for evacuation; Healy diverts for coring ops in E. Beaufort		
1	M	30-Aug	242	15:20	242	22:20	-7	Healy	Skirts Canadian EEZ; maximum incursion < 1 nmi		
1	M	30-Aug	242	18:26	243	1:26	-7	Healy	Skirts Canadian EEZ; maximum incursion < 1 nmi		
1	Tu	31-Aug	243	11:05	243	18:05	-7	Healy	4P-1 piston core and 4TC-1 trigger core on bottom (depth = 3,700 m)	75.58417°	140.09283°
1	Tu	31-Aug	243	18:30	244	1:30	-7	Louis	Medical evacuation of sick and injured crew members to Tuktoyuktuk by helicopter	70.25000°	133.75000°
1	Tu	31-Aug	243	22:23	244	5:23	-7	Healy	Healy enters Canadian EEZ for multibeam and sampling	74.72867°	137.41100°
1	W	1-Sep	244	1:00	244	8:00	-7	Louis	Underway from Tuktoyuktuk to rejoin Healy		

Joint U.S.-Canada 2010 Arctic UNCLOS Program

	Day of Week	Local Day	Local DOY	Local Time	UTC DOY	UTC (z)	UTC Delta	Vessel	Mission Chronology	Latitude N.	Longitude W.
1	W	1-Sep	244	21:00	245	4:00	-7	Louis	Louis enters heavy ice on return transit		
1	Th	2-Sep	245	11:36	245	18:36	-7	Healy	5P-1 piston core and 5TC-1 trigger core on bottom (depth = 2081 m)	76.54383°	128.62750°
1	Th	2-Sep	245	18:15	246	1:15	-7	both	Vessels rendezvous; Dept. of Homeland Security flyover	76.53517°	128.72750°
2	Th	2-Sep	245	19:00	246	2:00	-7	both	Deploy seismic gear, Healy in lead		
1	Sa	4-Sep	247	12:00	247	19:00	-7	Healy	Healy breaks off joint program to head to Barrow		
1	Sa	4-Sep	247	13:19	247	20:19	-7	Healy	Healy departs Canadian EEZ	75.77900°	136.76417°
1	Sa	4-Sep	247	17:00	248	1:00	-8	Healy	Change clocks to Alaskan daylight time zone		
1	Mo	6-Sep	249	4:00	249	12:00	-8	Healy	Arrive Barrow		
1	W	14-Sep	257	16:00	257	21:00	-5	Louis	Arrive Kugluktuk for disembarkation		

Data and Metadata

Extensive information regarding cruise HLY1002 (USGS Field Activity ID H-03-10-AR), including links to reports, articles, and blogs, is available at
http://walrus.wr.usgs.gov/infobank/h/h310ar/html/h-3-10-ar.meta.html

All raw data from the cruise are archived at the National Geophysical Data Center (NGDC) through the Rolling Deck to Repository initiative. Complete file manifests and other metadata are available at:
http://www.rvdata.us/catalog/HLY1002
http://get.rvdata.us/services/cruise/HLY1002.xml

Raw and processed multibeam data and metadata, as well as raw CHIRP subbottom data in SEG-Y format are posted on the NGDC's ECS data page at *http://ngdc.noaa.gov/mgg/ecs/cruises.html*. These data are also cross-posted at the Law of the Sea project's Web site at the Center for Coastal and Ocean Mapping of the University of New Hampshire's Law of the Sea repository at *http://ccom.unh.edu/theme/law-sea/arctic-ocean*.

IMPORTANT NOTE: Under terms of the Memorandum of Understanding between the USGS and the GSC, the swath-bathymetry and subbottom profile data acquired during cruise HLY1002 within the Canadian 200-nmi-wide Exclusive Economic Zone (EEZ) are proprietary, and public release is not presently authorized. The trackline segments that fall within the Canadian EEZ are listed in table 5.

Table 5. Time periods during which the *Healy* bathymetry and CHIRP subbottom data are embargoed until further notice.

Day	Date (UTC)	Julian day	UTC (Hour: Minute)	Comment	Latitude N.	Longitude W.
Sa	28-Aug	240	13:11	*Healy* enters Canadian EEZ for multibeam bathymetry.	81.38517°	122.99250°
M	30-Aug	242	7:47	*Healy* leaves Canadian EEZ.	79.51883°	131.64900°
Tu	31-Aug	244	5:23	*Healy* enters Canadian EEZ for multibeam bathymetry and sampling.	74.72867°	137.41100°
Sa	4-Sep	247	20:19	*Healy* leaves Canadian EEZ.	75.77900°	136.76417°

Public Outreach

Three members of the scientific party performed outreach duties, principally by writing expedition logs for different websites. Helen Gibbons (USGS) wrote for the ECS Project Web site (*http://continentalshelf.gov/missions/10arctic/*). Additional logs were written by two teachers on the scientific crew. William Schmoker, an Earth Science teacher at Centennial Middle School in Boulder, Colorado, joined the expedition through PolarTREC (*http://www.polartrec.com/*), a program that links teachers with researchers for hands-on field research in polar regions. Caroline Singler, an Earth Science and Aquatic Biology teacher at Lincoln Sudbury Regional High School in Sudbury, Massachusetts, joined the expedition through the National Oceanic and Atmospheric Administration (NOAA) Teacher at Sea program (*http://teacheratsea.noaa.gov/*), which places teacher-participants on research cruises run by NOAA and its partner agencies, such as the USGS.

Caroline Singler's log entries are available at *http://csinglertas.blogspot.com/*. In addition to teaching high school classes, Caroline coaches a National Ocean Sciences Bowl (NOSB) team, whose members followed her logs while she was at sea. Caroline's Earth Science class began near the end of the cruise, on August 31, 2010, allowing her to send a welcome from the Arctic to her new students. She used her log entries and data from the cruise in school exercises and NOSB coaching during the school year.

Bill Schmoker's log entries are posted at *http://www.polartrec.com/member/bill-schmoker*. Before the cruise, Bill was interviewed by a radio station and two newspapers in the Boulder area, alerting the community to the upcoming expedition and inviting them to follow his logs. Bill's Earth Science class began on August 18, 2010, giving the students about 2½ weeks to follow his log in near-real time from the Arctic. Bill also coordinated an event called PolarConnect: With the help of PolarTREC, his assistant principal, and the Coast Guard, he called Centennial Middle School from the *Healy* on August 31, 2010, spoke to two groups of about 300 students each, and engaged the students in question-and-answer sessions about the Arctic and his experiences there.

In addition to posting logs, the teachers assisted with watchstanding in the geophysics lab, processing sediment cores for storage, and collecting water subsamples for analysis aboard the *Healy* and at onshore labs. Their participation in the expedition provided practical help to the researchers onboard and spread information about the cruise and the ECS Project to students, teachers, parents, and the public in their communities.

Acknowledgments

We thank the entire crew of the USCG Cutter *Healy*, in particular Commanding Officer Captain William (Bill) J. Rall, Operations Officer Lieutenant Commander Eric St. Pierre, and Executive Officer Commander John Reeves. We are grateful for the planning and logistical support provided by David Forcucci, USCG liaison in Seattle.

We appreciate the dedication and expertise provided by the *Healy* technical-support team of Dale Chayes, Steve Roberts, and Tom Bolmer, who compiled the cruise data synopsis in appendix B. Bernie Coakley (University of Alaska, Fairbanks) processed the gravity data and provided the crossover analysis listed in table 2.

Florence Wong and Ray Sliter, USGS, reviewed the report.

This program was conducted under the auspices of the U.S. Extended Continental Shelf Task Force (*http://www.continentalshelf.gov/*).

References Cited

Childs, J.R., Triezenberg, P.J., and Danforth, W.W., 2012, 2008 Joint United States-Canadian Program to explore the limits of the Extended Continental Shelf aboard the U.S. Coast Guard Cutter *Healy*—Cruise HLY0806: U.S. Geological Survey Open-File Report 2012-1210, 15 p. and appendixes. (Also available at *http://pubs.usgs.gov/of/2012/1210/.*)

Coakley, Bernard, Kristoffersen, Yngve, and Hopper, John, 2005, Cruise report for underway geophysics program HLY 05-03 5—5 August 2005; Dutch Harbor, Alaska to 30 September, 2005; Tromso, Norway: Report to the U.S. National Science Foundation, 84 p., accessed February 13, 2012, at *http://www.icefloe.net/hly0503/HLY-05-03-MGG_Final_Report.pdf.*

Edwards, B.D., Saint-Ange, Frankie, Pohlman, John, Higgins, Jenna, Mosher, D.C., Lorenson, T.D., and Hart, Patrick, 2011, Sedimentology of cores recovered from the Canada Basin of the Arctic Ocean, Abstract PP33A-1915: Presented at 2011 Fall Meeting, American Geophysical Union, San Francisco, Calif., December 5–9, 2011

Grantz, Arthur, Hart, P.E., and May, S.D., 2004, Seismic reflection and refraction data acquired in Canada Basin, Northwind Ridge and Northwind Basin, Arctic Ocean in 1988, 1992 and 1993: U.S. Geological Survey Open-File Report 2004-1243. (Also available at *http://pubs.usgs.gov/of/2004/1243/.*)

Grantz, Arthur, May, S.D., and Mann, D.M., 1982, Tracklines of multichannel seismic-reflection data collected in the Beaufort and Chukchi Seas in 1977 for which demultiplexed field tapes are available from the U.S. Geological Survey: U.S. Geological Survey Open-File Report 82-651, 1 pl.

Hart, P.E., Pohlman, J.W., Lorenson, T.D., and Edwards, B.D., 2011, Beaufort Sea deep-water gas hydrate recovery from a seafloor mound in a region of widespread BSR occurrence: Proceedings of the 7th International Conference on Gas Hydrates (ICGH 2011), Edinburgh, Scotland, United Kingdom, July 17-21, 2011.

Hutchinson, D.R., Jackson, H.R., Shimeld, J.W., Chapman, C.B., Childs, J.R., Funck, T., and Rowland, R.W., 2009, Acquiring marine data in the Canada Basin, Arctic Ocean: EOS, Transactions, American Geophysical Union, v. 90, no. 23, p. 198–198.

Jackson, H.R., and DesRoches, K.J., 2010, 2008 Louis S. St-Laurent field report, August 22–October 3, 2008, Geological Survey of Canada, Open File 6275, 184 p., accessed February 13, 2013, a *ftp://ftp2.cits.rncan.gc.ca/pub/geott/ess_pubs/285/285359/of_6275.pdf.*

Kongsberg, 2010, Kongsberg EM series multibeam echo sounder, EM datagram formats: Kongsburg, Norway, Kongsberg Maritime AS, September 2010, 103 p., accessed March 13, 2013, at *http://www.km.kongsberg.com/ks/web/nokbg0397.nsf/AllWeb/253E4C58DB98DDA4C1256D7900483 73B/$file/160692_em_datagram_formats.pdf.*

Mayer, L.A., 2003, Cruise report—U.S. Law of the Sea cruise to map the foot of the slope and 2500-m isobath of the U.S. Arctic Ocean margin—Barrow, AK to Barrow. AK, August 30 to September 11, 2003: Durham, N.H., University of New Hampshire Center for Coastal and Ocean Mapping-Joint Hydrographic Center, 19 p., accessed February 14, 2013, at *http://ccom.unh.edu/sites/default/files/publications/Mayer_03_cruise_report_HE-0302.pdf.*

Mayer, L.A., 2004, Cruise report—U.S. Law of the Sea cruise to map theFfoot of the slope and 2500-m isobath of the U.S. Arctic Ocean margin— Nome, AK to Barrow, AK, October 6 to October 26, 2004: Durham, N.H., University of New Hampshire Center for Coastal and Ocean Mapping -Joint Hydrographic Center, 47 p., accessed February 14, 2012, at *http://ccom.unh.edu/sites/default/files/publications/Mayer_04_cruise_report_HE-0405.pdf.*

Mayer, L.A., and Armstrong, A.A., 2007, Cruise report—U.S. Law of the Sea cruise to map the foot of the slope and 2500-m Isobath of the U.S. Arctic Ocean margin—Barrow, AK to Barrow. AK, August 17 to September 15, 2007: Durham, N.H., University of New Hampshire Center for Coastal and

Ocean Mapping-Joint Hydrographic Center, 182 p., accessed February 14, 2013, at *http://ccom.unh.edu/sites/default/files/publications/Mayer_07_cruise_report_HE-0703.pdf.*

Mayer, L.A., and Armstrong, A.A., 2008, Cruise report—U.S. Law of the Sea cruise to map the foot of the slope and 2500-m isobath of the U.S. Arctic Ocean margin—Barrow, AK to Barrow, AK, August 14 to September 5, 2008: Durham, N.H., University of New Hampshire, Center for Coastal and Ocean Mapping-Joint Hydrographic Center, 179 p., accessed February 14, 2013, at *http://ccom.unh.edu/sites/default/files/publications/Mayer_08_HEALY_0805_CRUISERPT.pdf.*

Mayer, L.A., and Armstrong, A.A., 2009, Cruise report—U.S. Law of the Sea cruise to map the foot of the slope and 2500-m isobath of the US Arctic Ocean margin—Barrow, AK to Barrow, AK, August 7 to September 16, 2009 : Durham, N.H., University of New Hampshire Center for Coastal and Ocean Mapping-Joint Hydrographic Center, 118 p., accessed February 14, 2013, at *http://ccom.unh.edu/sites/default/files/publications/Mayer_2009_cruise_report_HE0905.pdf.*

Mayer, L.A. and Armstrong, A.A., 2011, Cruise report—U.S. Law of the Sea cruise to map the foot of the slope and 2500-m isobaths of the U.S. Arctic Ocean margin—Barrow, AK to Dutch Harbor, AK, August 15 to September 28, 2011: Durham, N.H., University of New Hampshire Center for Coastal and Ocean Mapping-Joint Hydrographic Center, 235 p., accessed February 14, 2013, at *http://ccom.unh.edu/sites/default/files/publications/Mayer_2011_cruise_report_HEALY1102.pdf.*

Mosher, D.C., ed., 2012, 2011 Canadian high Arctic Seismic Expedition—CCGS Louis S. St-Laurent cruise report: Geological Survey of Canada, Open File 7053; 290 p., doi: 10.4095/290241, accessed March 13, 2013, at *ftp://ftp2.cits.rncan.gc.ca/pub/geott/ess_pubs/290/290241/of_7053.pdf.*

Mosher, D.C., Shimeld, J.W., Chapman, C.B., 2011, 2010 Canada Basin seismic reflection and refraction survey, western Arctic Ocean—CCGS Louis S. St-Laurent expedition report: Geological Survey of Canada, Open File 6720; 252 p., accessed March 13, 2013, at [*ftp://ftp2.cits.rncan.gc.ca/pub/geott/ess_pubs/288/288024/of_6720.pdf*].

Mosher, D.C., Shimeld, J.W., and Hutchinson, D.R., 2009, 2009 Canada Basin seismic reflection and refraction survey, western Arctic Ocean—CCGS Louis S. St-Laurent expedition report: Geological Survey of Canada, Open File 6343, 266 p., accessed March 13, 2013, at *ftp://ftp2.cits.rncan.gc.ca/pub/geott/ess_pubs/248/248208/of_6343.pdf*].

Wan, Elmyra, McGann, M.L., and Edwards, B.D., 2011, Preliminary planktic and benthic foraminiferal biostratigraphy of cores from the Canada Basin, western Arctic Ocean, Abstract PP33A-1916: Presented at 2011 Fall Meeting, American Geophysical Union, San Francisco, Calif., December 5–9, 2011.

Appendices

Appendixes can be accessed and downloaded at http://pubs.usgs.gov/of/2013/1067.

Appendix A. Cruise-level Metadata

Appendix B. Data Synopsis (Chayes, Bolmer and Roberts)

Appendix C. Digital Data Formats

Appendix D. Geophysical Watchstander E-logs

Appendix E. Coring Operations Deck Logs

Appendix F. Water Sampling and Ocean Acidification Measurements

Appendix G . Protected Species Observer Report

Appendix H. Polar Bear Interaction Plan